Innocence and Fatigues

John H Olcott

John H Olcott

Copyright © 2016 John H. Olcott

All rights reserved. No part of this book may All be reproduced, stored, or transmitted by any means---- whether auditory, graphic, mechanical, or electronic- --- without written permission of both publisher and author, except in cases of brief excerpes used and crircal articles and reviews. Unauthorize reproduction of any part of this work is illegal and punishable by law

This is based on a true story. Some of the characters names have been changed to protect their privacy, incidents, organizations and dialogue in this novel are to the best of the author's recollection.

All rights reserved.

ISBN-13: 978-1535447218

ISBN-10: 1535447214

Available from Amazon.com, CreateSpace.com, and other retail outlets

DEDICATION

I would like to dedicate this writing to a small girl named Su Lee and all the innocent civilians who happened to be in the wrong place at the wrong time.

John H Olcott

CONTENTS

Acknowledgments	
Off to War	7
Appeasing the War God	13
All Wounds Can't be Seen	21
Goodbye Wasn't Heard	29
Darkness Without Night	37
The Flagpole	43

ACKNOWLEDGMENTS

I first have to acknowledge my Lord and Savior Jesus Christ for getting me through that war.

I also would like to acknowledge my two daughter-in-law's Sky and Tina for editing this work.

And lastly the rest of my family Joan, Jeff, Jody, Julie and Jason for putting up with me for all these years

John H Olcott

forward

I have written this as a small portion of history. I hope that the readers of its contents would be able to see and feel the emotional battle that one may go through, if they or their loved ones are sent off to war. I also have documented this for my children and grandchildren and perhaps their children; what it was like for me to go to war. This is a very small portion of my one year tour in Vietnam; the rest of my story may or may not be written.

I have changed the names of many of the characters to honor their privacy. The names that I have not changed, was to honor their presence.

Bob, the main character, was drafted and sent to Vietnam along with the other 2 million young men for the length of that war. He served his one-year tour with the First Cavalry Division. He was assigned to Company B, in the First Battalion of the Fifth Regiment. This was an infantry rifle company. He was commonly called a "grunt." The only position in the military that was lower than his, were the guys who had the duty of burning the waste material which they had to remove from the latrines.

Go back in time with this innocent teenage, Bob and walk with him in his footsteps to manhood.

Chapter One

Off to War

It's hard to imagine that I am writing about an event that happened fifty years ago. So, come with me as I go back in time to 1967. Our country was fully committed to the Vietnam conflict where 200,000 soldiers were on the ground in a country the size of Florida.

A young nineteen-year-old American soldier by the name of Bob Apple was one of them. He was doing his best to stay alive in spite of everything around him trying to inflict pain upon him; everything from the unforgiving jungle, with its elephant grass that would rip his flesh and his fatigues to shreds, to mosquitoes carrying the deadly malaria virus, snakes of all kinds, and rats the size of cats.

The enemy, which he was fighting, was very skilled in guerrilla warfare. They had been fighting the French for many years before we, the Americans, had arrived. Their hit and run tactics were extremely effective, along with the endless number of booby-traps which were not designed to kill but instead were designed with the intent to create serious wounds which disrupted our daily missions. We had to wait for a medevac chopper to remove the wounded.

Now if Bob did see his enemy, it was to create fear in the hearts of Bob and his brothers in arms. They were greatly outnumbered by an enemy whose greatest honor would be dying for their country. Bob and his buddies goal was to go home and go back to school, or raise a family, even with a 50% chance of being killed, or a 75% chance of being wounded.

Bob was in an infantry company; he was called a grunt in the First Calvary Division.

He was now living in a third world country. The villages which he was doing patrols through were extremely primitive. The homes consisted of a ten by twelve bamboo walls, palm branches for a roof, and dirt floors. Water was carried from streams or pulled out of wells with a rope and bucket and cooking was done over an open flame.

As Bob walk through these villages, he would see women openly nursing their young, older women smiling showing their blackened teeth caused by the effect of chewing beetle nut. The beetle nut was used as a drug to ease their mental and physical pain. The younger children played with no diapers. All the young men within fighting age were gone, leaving a very small workforce of young children and old men to work the rice paddies. They had their water buffalo and homemade wooden plows for most of the heavy work.

The simplicity of their lives lay on a green palm leaf in the form of a handful of cooked rice.

This was quite a contrast to the American dream, which Bob was living six months ago; no concern for transportation or all the conveniences that electricity provided for him. To be comfortable in any type of weather, and having leisure time to enjoy with family and friends.

After living in the fields and jungle for the past six months, Bob had almost become used to sleeping on the ground in the mud and cold during the rainy seasons, or battling the insects trying to bite him in the middle of the heated night all while pulling his night watch every two hours so his buddies could get some sleep. Bob was always waiting for the night darkness to explode with sudden death from gunfire. He sat praying for the morning sunrise. Then waking up to one less day to serve in this hellhole. Never knowing when he would be receiving his next hot meal made it only harder to saddle up and carry more than his own weight on his back for the next eight to fifteen hours through an unforgiving jungle. With every step wondering if that one might be his last. Then hearing the words passed down the line, "Change of mission. We are going to be air lifted to a hot LZ. A Company has made contact with the enemy and they need our help."

He had accepted the realization that this would be the norm for the next six months. Bob became callous to the threat of death around him. But one of the things that he did have a hard time dealing with was putting his severely wounded buddies on the medevac choppers and never knowing if they lived or died.

Morale in Bob's company was low, they were told that the only difference between the animals in the jungle and them was, that they can and will shave. Bob chose not to.

Bob's company commander requested a break for the company which was granted. Around May 20, the company set up to guard the bridge on Highway 14, which stretched over the Giang River. The company was set up in various locations up and down the river. This was the third time that Bob has been at this location. This would be a time of rest and relaxation for Bob and the company. A hot meal once a day and a resupply of ammo, cigarettes and C rations were being distributed, until the mailbag was seen. It has been six weeks since they have received any mail from home. The war seemed to stop, as they all sat and smelled the aroma of those perfumed soak envelopes which contained news from home; some good, some bad.

Being set up by the river Bob had the opportunity to bathe and wash his clothes. Swimming was allowed as long as our guards were posted. Across the highway there was a field that was big enough to play baseball in. The ball was made of rolling three pairs of socks in to a ball, and a stick was the bat.

The children from the nearby village of Ben Giang would come and beg for food and played baseball with us. There were about eight or ten of the same children that would come every day and had been coming the last two times Bob was there. One little girl, Bob nicknamed Su Lee, had taken a liking to Bob. He too was caught up in the dilemma that she posed to him. This little six or seven-year-old girl who was extremely bright, spoke English well enough to carry on conversations. She had an overwhelming desire to learn to read English and try to get anyone to teach her to read. Most of the other guys did not want these little beggars around. They all had their reasons to justify their stance. Bob could not resist doing something kind in this world they were in, filled with hate and death. Bob was trying to convince some of the other guys to start a fund to send her to school because there was no public school system; only children of wealthy parents were allowed to attend school. So when Bob was not assigned any duties, he could be found sitting in the shade with Su Lee teaching her to read or doing math.

Su Lee was responsible enough that her mother, at times, would allow her to bring her three-year-old brother with her. She had also told Bob that her father was a soldier too but in the South Vietnam Army.

John H Olcott

Chapter Two

Appeasing the War God

On the morning of May 22 the morning seemed no different than it had been the days before. There was a gentle breeze blowing up the river, blowing the tops of the palm trees, which shaded its banks. It was going to be another hot day; most of the guys have already removed their shirts along with Bob. The children arrived a little later than normal. The North Vietnamese Army had raided their village last night and stole their rice supply. Most of the villagers were up all night in fear of their return. There were only five or six children that came and Su Lee was one of them. She tried to be strong as she told Bob about how the bad soldiers came to their home looking for food and told her mother not to make a sound or they would kill her. Bob wanted to get her mind off of the events of the night before. He got out one of his letters he received from home. She could smell the perfume that Bob's girlfriend had soaked the envelope in. Su Lee laughed and said, "She loves you." He read what he could to her, and she knew he was just making stuff up to make her feel better.

A group of guys and the other children were going across the road to play baseball. Bob convinced her to play baseball with them before a reading lesson, which she agreed to. Bob carefully folded up his letter and put it in a plastic bag with his other letters from home. This was his way of trying to keep his lifeline to the real world dry. Su Lee started across the road as Bob finish putting the letters in his rucksack.

There was very little traffic on the road, mostly people walking and a few riding bicycles. As Bob walked quickly to meet up with her in the center of the road he heard something hitting the pavement behind him. Su Lee turned first and looked at the object that was thrown. Bob could tell by the look in her eyes, that something wasn't right. Bob turned quickly to see a hand grenade lying within five feet of them. Another soldier by the name of Larry Lach was moving up behind him. Bob's first thought was this must be the fake grenade like the ones the guys would use to get all the civilians out of the buses faster allowing them to check ID's before crossing the bridge. Bob would not give into their cruel joke. He turned to assure Su Lee that it wasn't real. Su Lee was reaching forward to grab Bob's hand. The same instant as their fingertips touched and their eyes met Bob could see the bright explosion in her brown eyes.

He was blown away from her with the blast that violently left him in a state of shock. It was real, flashed through his head, and I'm not dead. As he looked around to see if they were under attack, he could see Doc Gonzales running over to Larry who was lying in a pool of blood. His next thought was Su Lee. She was laying ten feet away from him now. Bob quickly ran over to her and picked up her lifeless body. By this time the rest of the guys were in defensive positions around us. Bob yelled for Doc Gonzalez to come over to help her. He yelled back that he couldn't leave Larry.

Bob's mind raced to remember the first aid techniques he was taught. Stop the bleeding clear her airway. Her airway was clear. Her breathing was shallow as she moaned in pain. Stopping her bleeding would be extremely challenging. The blast had thrown hundreds of pieces of scrap metal into her little body embedding pieces of her clothing into her wounds. Her clothes drenched in blood. The 'god of war' wanted this sacrifice. Bob looked at the small first-aid bandage that was attached to his gun belt knowing it would be useless. He yelled to the guys to bring towels to wrap her in. The same towels that were being used for bases on the ball field or used to wipe the sweat off of their faces just two minutes before. Bob fought with the devil trying to save the life of this innocent little girl. He sat and rocked her little body telling her it would be okay once the helicopters arrived. In the distance he could hear the choppers coming. He could now feel her blood soaking through his pants. She was no longer moaning and Bob was afraid to unwrap her to see if she was alive. He kept her covered as the choppers landed throwing dust and dirt all over her blood soaked towels. Doc went on the first chopper with Larry, and Bob carried Su Lee to the other chopper and put her on board. His arms and the entire front of him were covered with her blood. He turned and started walking to the river to clean up. The gunner from the chopper caught him and told him to get on board. "You are hit," he said as he pointed to Bob's back. Bob climbed on the chopper and sat away from her. Looking down at her as she laid on the dark diamond plate steel floor of the chopper, he hoped that he hadn't lost this battle, as he watched the attending medic start her IV.

Bob's mind was being filled with questions that there were no answers too. Why did Larry get 90% of the blast and not him? Who threw the grenade? Would Su Lee's parents be notified? Why would this 'god of war' want this innocent child?

A place that was supposed to be restful and relaxing is now turning into an emotional roller coaster ride for Bob. The shock of what has just happened must be wearing off. He was now starting to feel the bee stings in his back, and other parts of his body where the grenade fragments had penetrated. It was a short ride to the hospital in Chu Lai. After the chopper had landed Bob was able to walk to the location of their first aid station. He never looked back to say goodbye to her or to find out if she was alive or dead. His very soul was filled with hate and bitterness; he would never get that close to anyone again.

After going through the triage, most of his scrap metal wounds were small except for the one on his hand. He tried to convince them that all he needed was a couple of bandages and that he would be good to go. He wanted to go back to his company before they found out that this would be his third Purple Heart and find some cushy job for him in the rear. They told him that he had to stay a couple days and be on antibiotics to help fight off the infections. He was assigned a bed and given a hospital gown; and told where the showers were. Tonight he would be sleeping on a soft bed with a pillow and on clean sheets, something his body has not felt in six months. As he passed by the beds in the ward, all the guys were looking at him as he passed by. Still in his blood soaked pants and his stomach and arms covered in dried blood, his back look like a dot-to-dot game with all the little holes of where the shrapnel had penetrated his back.

It wasn't until he was in the shower, a real shower with tile walls and floor that he stood and watched the physical part of his war being washed down the drain. Watching all the blood that Su Lee so desperately needed being wasted. It wasn't until then that he realized how close he was to his own death. Why had God spared him? For the first time in six months Bob's emotions got the best of him. He began to cry. All the horrors of the war passed before his eyes. He was actually surprised that he had made it six months. Then his thoughts drifted to his buddies he was leaving behind. Yes, they would be getting hot meals tonight like he would, but they would still be sleeping on the ground, bathing in dirty river water, not knowing what the night might bring. They would be one man short pulling watch tonight. Now his name would be listed on a casualty report with some wounds that will never be seen.

After drying himself off and slipping into the hospital gown Bob was unable to tie the strings on the back because of his hand. He carried his blood soaked pants and boots, the only possessions that he had left to show for the last six months of his life. All of his letters and his camera with six rolls of undeveloped film, and his lucky shirt with the bullet hole in the left shoulder were all left behind. He walked to the nurse's station to see how long of a wait he would have before they could have a closer look at his hand.

A nurse came up behind him and asked in a very pleasant way if he needed some help tying his gown. She told him that his wife or girlfriend wouldn't like him to be parading around like that, as she pointed to his bare butt. It was not until that instance that Bob realized he had no room in his life for any embarrassment or any other feeling; he was numb.

They wrapped some gauze around his hand and bandaged it to stop the bleeding. They told him to just go rest at his bed and they would get to him when they could.

This was a busy place; it was part recovery room and part triage. Some of the guys were not as fortunate as Bob. They were waking up to the shock of missing body parts. They finally got to him and told him that he would have to have hand surgery in Japan. The tendon in one of his fingers was three quarters torn through. He knew his chances of going back to the company in the next couple days were gone. He would not have a chance to say goodbye to his buddies.

While lying on his clean sheets his head was surrounded by the comfort of his pillow. His brain was starting to be filled with overwhelming guilt. His body was enjoying the comfort that it have not felt in some time. And the fresh smell of soap on the sheets lingered in the air. Yet his brain would not let him enjoy these comforts. At one point he almost had himself convinced that he would sleep better if he were on the floor next to his bed. Knowing that the nurses would not allow it, he remained in bed and wrestled with all those questions that he had no answers to earlier in the day. He kept seeing the fear and the explosion in Su Lee's eyes, over and over again. Now he was angry with himself for not staying with her when they arrived. He will probably never know if she became another sacrifice to this cruel 'god of war'.

This cruel and wicked god thrives on the blood of its innocent victims. And will not be happy until there is no more body part to be taken. He does not recognize gender, race or the color of your skin, soldier or civilian. He will not stop until the last shot is fired. No matter how hard you try to fight this unseen enemy you will lose. He will always win, and laugh at those who try to defeat him.

In spite of being in one of the most secure places he has been in since he arrived in Vietnam, he could not sleep. He waited for the night nurse to come by, and asked her for some more pain pills and something to help him sleep. He really wasn't in much pain, but was hoping the combination of the two would help wash away his thoughts. It wasn't too long after receiving the pills and he was dozing off into a world that he would be fighting the rest of his life.

Chapter Three

All Wounds Can't be Seen

The following morning Bob found himself on a plane heading for the 106 Army medical Hospital in Yokohama Japan. Before leaving he was issued some new army fatigues and boots. His back was covered with small circular bandages; his right leg was sporting a larger bandage, which covered a place where a larger piece of shrapnel went through. They also had his left hand completely wrapped giving the impression that his hand injury was a lot worse than it really was. This was not a commercial flight. The plane was a medical transport with cot like bunk beds in the center rows for the severely wounded. Along the walls there were cargo strap seats.

Bob tried to make himself comfortable in spite of his feelings of being out of place. To be surrounded by soldiers who had sacrificed body parts. In spite of the severity of their wounds, their spirits were high, knowing that this flight was the first leg of their journey back to the states. Their war seemed to be over. Now Bob was to fight a new war, one in which he had never been trained. Where his own mind would be his biggest enemy.

After landing in Yokohama, the patients on litters were transported to the hospital by ambulance. A bus transported Bob and those who could walk. Once arriving at the hospital he handed his medical records along with any x-rays he had to the triage nurse. He was assigned to a ward, which would be his home for the next four to six weeks.

There were at least twenty beds in this ward and they were all full. Bob's bed sat between one fella who had been shot three times in the abdomen. The fellow on the other side was a double amputee and was missing part of his right hand. No consideration was made in the severity of anyone's condition in regard to what ward they were assigned to. Once a bed became available the next patient in line got it. Bob tried to settle in to this uncomfortable situation. Since his wounds were probably one of the least of these other twenty guys. He tried to become their caregivers. Until one night the fellow with the stomach wounds was moved back to intensive care. Bob's mind was shutting down he couldn't lose another one. During the daytime hours Bob could no longer stay in the ward and care for the sick. He was given a day pass so he could go into town every day, just as long as he got back in time for his hand therapy appointments.

The second day he was in Yokohama he bumped into another guy from his ward. They spent most of the afternoon in a bar trying to find out how much sake' it would take to erase the war. Whatever portion of the war that was erased in the afternoon, was brought back to life that evening, hearing the moans and groans of the severely wounded in his Ward. Bob missed the quietness of the nights in the jungle.

The following day, after his morning therapy, Bob met up with Eddie the fella from his ward. They planned on lunch and a movie. Bob wanted to see more of Yokohama than the inside of a bar. They found a nice restaurant in the midst of the business district downtown. Per Bob's request the hostess sat them in a booth near the back of the restaurant. Bob sat with his back to the wall, so that the front door was in his full view. It was lunch hour for many of the businesses in the area, and the restaurant was beginning to fill up. They were watching the patrons as they were eating their meals with some sort of sense of urgency, not seeming to enjoy the flavor of their food, but to eat out of necessity. Bob and Eddie were going to enjoy every mouthful of the hot meal that they have ordered.

Bob couldn't help noticing too young Japanese women looking in the front window to see if there were any empty tables. The waitress was clearing off the booth right next to theirs. One of the girls pointed towards the booth, at the same time grabbing the shoulder of the other girl who was turning to walk away. Bob asked Eddie "if he believed in angels,"while pointing to the front door. Eddie turned to see what Bob was looking at. As Eddie turned back around, with a smile from ear to ear saying, "with our luck they'll be married." The hostess was escorting the two young ladies to the booth next to them; Bob was beaming in the possibilities of what these two beautiful young ladies meant. A chance of leaving the war behind, if just for a little while in Bob's eyes they represented everything good and tender. Full of innocence, a world that Bob wanted to go back to. Both of the girls cordially smiled at them as they were seated. Bob could not take his eyes off of the one who wore her hair tied up in a bun exposing her long neck. He wanted to strike up a conversation with them, but all the guilt from the past six months was swimming in his head. How dare he enjoy the company of this girl, knowing his buddies may be dying in some rice paddy? Eddie was not going to pass up this opportunity. He asked them if they spoke any English. The other girl, who had long flowing shiny black hair, nodded her head yes. He asked them if they knew where the closest theater was. One thing led to the next and before their meal was delivered the girls were sharing the booth with Bob and Eddie.

Bob had a hard time believing that these two beautiful young ladies would be interested in two GIs.

They were professionals who worked in a bank, one as a teller and the other as a loan officer. They had introduced themselves as Lynn and Setsuko. Lynn had long black hair and Setsuko wore her hair on top of her head. They were free thinkers trying to learn as much as they could about United States. They were dressed in short skirts and blouses, high heels and nylons, just like the girls were back in the states. The Western influence was spreading through Japan. Mainly the women over forty were still wearing their silk kimonos. Eddie invited them to go to the movie with us. They declined but said they would be free the following day, which was Saturday. They made arrangements to meet up with them in front of the theater the next day.

The rest of the day Bob had mixed emotions. He wondered why these beautiful girls were interested in them. Was he going to be nothing more than a ticket for them to the United States? Or was Setsuko just as interested in him as a person as he was of her. At this point it didn't matter, the excitement of the upcoming day was enough to lift his spirits. That evening as he pillow his head, thinking of his buddies who were not as fortunate as he, and hearing the moans of the guys in the ward. He couldn't help but think of Setsuko and the scent of her perfume. The harder he tried to erase her thoughts, more disloyal he felt towards his girlfriend back home and his buddies in the field.

The next morning Eddie met up with him right after breakfast, to discuss the plans for the day. He tried to explain to Eddie about his feelings of disloyalty, and that he would rather pass on seeing the girls.

Eddie would have none of it, he told Bob "he didn't have to marry the girl, just pretend it was his sister."

Bob agreed to tag along; he never knew at that time how much he needed Setsuko in his life. They went to the movie that afternoon followed by dinner. Lynn and Eddie after dinner decided to go to a bar for some drinks. Leaving Setsuko and Bob to enjoy the city lights. Setsuko spoke very little English and Bob spoke no Japanese at all. In spite of the language difficulty they seem to enjoy one another's company. She gave Bob a map of the train system, and showed him where she lived.

On the train ride she tries to hold his hand. He did not want to offend her so he allowed her to do so. In spite of the fact that he knew he should stop seeing her. He asked if he could see her the following day. Which led to seeing her almost every day for the next four weeks. She had become the medicine that he needed. She had accepted him for who he was, not who he thought he was. He was able to confide in her his deepest emotions. In spite of the language barrier she knew what he was feeling, and wrapped her arms around him, her warmth and tenderness spoke volumes.

Lynn and Eddie did not get past the first night, it seemed Eddie wanted more than a movie and a dinner. For a while Setsuko would bring Lynn alone as an interpreter. It was during those times that he found out that Setsuko had been living a very sheltered life. Her father did not allow her to date very much, and was not in approval of his daughter seeing a GI. Bob wanted to meet her parents, and asked if he would be able to come to her home for dinner. The arrangements were made for the next Saturday night.

When that evening arrived Bob was trying to remember all the Japanese greetings that he has learned. There he stood at the front door in his freshly pressed khakis and spit shined boots, his service hat was tucked under his left arm. He knocked softly on the door, and was expecting her father to be the one opening it. To his surprise Setsuko greeted him. She was dressed in a silk kimono wearing white socks, and her hair was tied up a bun. She instructed Bob to remove his boots, and escorted him into the dining area.

The home was very simple and carries the tradition of a Japanese home. It was decorated with bright reds, yellow and brown objects.

As her father entered the room Setsuko lowered her head saying something to her father in Japanese as she pointed to Bob. That was Bob's cue to bend gently at the waste and greet her father in Japanese, which they have been rehearsing for the last couple days. Setsuko's father, whose name was Juro, gesture to Bob to sit on the pillow to his left. The seating arrangements at the table, which was maybe fourteen inches off the floor; there were pillows for chairs. Setsuko and her mother sat directly across from Bob. He was now seeing a different side to Setsuko that he had never seen before. She and her mother were extremely reverent of her father. No one started eating until her father started, and when he was finished, so were they.

Once again the meals seem like a necessity of life, rather than an experience.

The women quickly cleared the table off. A box of dominoes was placed in the center of the table, and Juro said in broken English "you play." They both smiled at one another, and the girls covered their mouths as they giggled.

The rest of the evening went well. Bob's train ride back to the hospital was filled with thoughts of how much he really cared for Setsuko. She was awakening feelings that he thought he had lost. She was so extremely different from his girlfriend back home. He still wonder why this beautiful, intelligent young lady, would want to be around him. He knew it could be just a matter of days before his orders would be coming down and he would be leaving. He tried to push those thoughts out of his mind. While sitting back with his eyes close, smelling the scent of her perfume, which was left on his clothing.

Chapter Four

Goodbye Wasn't Heard

The train ride seems shorter than normal. He was now back witnessing the remnants of war. Billy, the double amputee in the bed next to him was having a horrible night. He asked Bob if he would scratch his missing feet again, to see if it would ease his pain. Bob had enough pain of his own, which could not be seen. After watching Su Lee suffering and possibly dying in his arms, he said he would never get close to anyone again. He wonder why he aloud Setsuko to get so close. Maybe he could come back after his tour was over. His life has become more complicated now than it was when only had to think about was staying alive. He asked the night nurse if he could have some more pills for sleep.

The next morning after coming back to the ward from breakfast. The atmosphere in the ward was very still and quiet. As he approached his bed, he could see the reason for the quietness. His orders were lying on the bed. Everyone in the room knew where he was going. His eyes frantically race through the orders to the part that said destination, Cam Ranh

Bay Vietnam; his wounds were not severe enough to warrant him going back to the states. Going back to that war-torn country, and possibly facing death again did not bother him as much as leaving Setsuko. His flight would be leaving 6 AM Tuesday morning, which meant all day Monday would be clearing the hospital until dinner that evening.

He wasn't supposed to meet up with Setsuko at the train station in Yokohama until noon. He decided he would meet her at the station by her house, giving him one more hour with her. He arrived at the station one hour before she would be getting on the train. While sitting and trying to figure out exactly how and when he was going to tell her that he would be leaving. Not wanting to ruin their day together he decided he would tell her after dinner that evening. Looking around the train station a brochure about an art gallery caught his eye. He thought that would get his mind off of him leaving and gives them something to do today.

Sitting on the bench outside the station door watching the people coming and going and the war that he would be going back to was nowhere to be seen.

His eyes caught Setsuko as she was approaching the station. He now noticed more than ever all the wonderful things about her that he never told her like the bounce in her hair when she walks, when it was down. She'd made her choice of clothing look elegant. As she walked, she carried herself with grace and dignity. Her smile and laughter seemed to have melted Bob's heart. He tried to push down his feelings. Could he be in love with a woman that he has never kissed? The harder he tried not to like her, the closer they became. She was indeed the medicine that he needed at that time. She was able to gently massage his feelings to the surface again, without him even knowing it.

As Bob stood up, she seen him and ran to greet him. With a big pleasant smile, wrapping her arms around him, and looking at him through her deep chocolate brown eyes. She said "you happy me" in her broken English, as she squeezed him harder. They spent the rest of the day at the art gallery. Each time that Setsuko would laugh or smile that sent a knife through his heart. Knowing that some time that evening he would have to tell her. He now was aware that she was not looking for just some GI as a ticket to America. He thought all afternoon of how he could tell her without hurting her. He was not going to spoil the rest of the day trying to figure out what to tell her. He did decide a better location would be at the train station.

During dinner Setsuko had noticed that Bob was different and had asked if she had did something wrong. Unconsciously Bob was trying to push her away, trying to protect himself from his own pain. He made up some story about one of the new guys who came in was from his company, and he was in pretty bad shape. After dinner walking hand and hand to the train station they discussed that they would meet for dinner Monday evening at the station here by her house. They arrived at the station thirty minutes before Bob's train would be going back to Yokohama.

Bob sat Setsuko on the bench outside the station. Standing in front of her he reached down and grabbed both her hands. He was now feeling the same frightening feeling in his stomach that he did when they were flying into a hot LZ.

She gazed up at him and saw the look on his face. Squeezing his hands she said "what's wrong."

Staring into her eyes Bob mumbled "I have to go back."

As her eyes filled with tears, she let go of Bob's hands, stood up and started to walk away.

Bob could not let her go like this. He went over and wrapped his arms around her hoping her sodding would stop. In between her crying she was able to ask "when."

He pointed to the calendar on the station wall as he put his finger on Tuesday and said "morning."

The pain of him leaving was almost more than she could bear. She beat her fist on his chest, as she repeatedly said "no, no, no."

He was finally able to quiet her down.

She sat next to him in a state of shock, as he was trying to tell her that they both knew this day would finally come.

She tried to be strong as she said, "To soon."

Bob's train was pulling into the station and he would have to leave. He told her he would see her tomorrow evening as he wiped a tear from her cheek.

He began to say "goodbye", but she stopped him by putting her finger on his lips. Bob quickly found a seat by the window so he would be able to see her on the platform. There she stood still in the state of shock, with her hand only raised to shoulder height to wave goodbye.

Bob's Monday drag with all the meaningless exams and papers that he had to sign so he would be able to leave the hospital and go back to the war zone. The only bright spot of the day would be him seeing Setsuko that evening. He went to the PX and bought a necklace for her. He pondered with the thought of telling her that after the war, he would come back for her. Then he thought what if he was killed, she would never know.

The entire train ride to her home was filled with excitement; there would be no surprises. He was going to tell her his feelings. As the train slowly pulled into her station Bob looked on the platform for Setsuko, she was nowhere to be found. This was not like her; she was always on time. Then he recognizes Lynn walking up to him.

Bob fumbled around for the words to speak that might consume all of his thoughts. Then he just said with a voice louder than he should, "where is she," thinking the worst.

Lynn motioned for him to sit down. She proceeded to tell him, that Setsuko would not be coming; she could not bear the thought of saying goodbye to you. She has beautiful thoughts of you that she will keep in her heart forever. She does not want you to see her cry anymore.

Bob told Lynn that he was going to her home. I have to say "goodbye to her, and tell her I love her."

Lynn stopped him, and told him she wouldn't be home. Lynn looked him directly in the eyes and said, "do you really think she doesn't know how much you care for her."

Bob was caught totally off guard; he needed some time to process this.

Lynn stayed with Bob until his train arrived; reaching for his ticket he found the necklace. He handed the necklace to Lynn, and asked her to give it to Setsuko.

She then gave Bob an envelope and told him not to read it until the train left the station. Lynn smiled, and said "Setsuko told me what to write." After putting the envelope in his pocket he gave Lynn a big hug, he told her thank you [in Japanese].

The train seems to be moving slower than usual. Bob reached in his pocket and pulled out the envelope, which carry the aroma of Setsuko perfume. He carefully opened it and unfolded the paper. There were only four words written in English and Setsuko signature, in Japanese. Bob almost knew what she had written before he opened the envelope. They had spent so much time together without speaking that they almost knew what the other was thinking. His thoughts were drifting back to his buddies in Vietnam and what battles he may be facing as he returns. But he will always have the memories of falling in love with a Japanese girl that he had never kissed.

Tuesday morning, Bob was on a bus in route to the airport. None of the bus passengers were talking. They all had the same thing in common; in a matter of minutes they would be loading the plane heading back to Vietnam.

His thoughts were on Setsuko, he wonders if she would find enough strength to show up to say goodbye. The bus slowed down and stopped at the guard station just outside the airport. No civilians were being allowed beyond this point. Bob anxiously look to see if she might be there. Two guys went over and opened the windows on the curbside of the bus. Their girlfriends ran to them, trying to touch their lovers for one last time. The MPs had to pull the crying girls away, as the bus slowly drove through the gate. Bob sat in silence remembering Setsuko's tears running down her face. He had to try now to forget her, and push her out of his mind. He could not be distracted with thoughts about her where he was going.

Now after recovering in Japan for six weeks. He was on a flight back to a war zone in Vietnam, to finish his last five months of service. After the plane had landed in Cam Ranh Bay, Vietnam. All of its passengers were ushered into a large building. The Sgt. in charge, barked out Bob's name along with two others. He gave them directions to a lieutenant colonels office; they were told that he would be waiting for their arrival. Bob knew that if someone in the Army knew your name; and especially an officer, you are probably in trouble. Fortunately this wasn't the case. All three of them have been awarded three purple hearts. They wanted Bob to take a job as an MP in Saigon, a more secure duty, but Bob refused and asked to go back to his old company. They granted him that request.

Bob was hoping that someday the company might return to the same bridge and he would be able to visit with Su Lee's mother to see if she was now chewing beetle nut to ease her pain.

Chapter Five

Darkness Without Night

The following day, Bob returned to his company base camp in An Khe. While he was reporting into the company's clerk, the clerk told Bob that he thought he would never see him again. "I'm glad you're back; the new guys can sure use your help out there." He told Bob about June 21, how the company was penned down all day and half of the night. We had ten kills and over forty wounded. More than half of the company is gone. Bob's heart sunk in his chest. A feeling of guilt and shame was covering him like a big black cloud. One of his biggest fears while he was in hospital was now a reality. He was falling in love, and sleeping on clean sheets while his buddies were dying in some dirty rice paddy.

Not wanting to know anymore. He went to his barracks. The last time he was here it was back in December. The barracks were tents with dirt floors then. Now there were wooden walls about two foot tall, which sat on a cement floor. The remainders of the walls were screens to allow for good ventilation and the roof was tin with a large overhang, to shed the monsoon rains. Bob open the screen door and went into this fine structure.

He looked at all the metal bunks and mattresses that have not been slept on. Duffel bags were guarding at the head of each bed. The new bags look crisp and clean, as they sat with hopes of going home with their owners, and not leaving with the sorrow and grief of bad news. It was easy to determine all the new replacements bags, compared to the old-timers. Bob has now earned the rank of being called an old-timer. So he looked for a bag with molds on the bottom. After finding his bag and bed he just sat and wondered what kind of a battle had the company been in to lose so many guys.

The clerk was coming in the building with some sheets and a pillow for him.

He said, "I know this will not be as comfortable as the hospital, but I will try to keep you here as long as I can."

Bob replied, "No need to, the first chopper headed to the company tomorrow, I'll be on it."

"You can keep the sheets and pillow clean, I won't need them."

"Suit yourself" the clerk replied as he sat on the bed across from Bob.

Bob asked, "who were the guys killed," without thinking. Hoping they wouldn't be anyone that he was close to. The clerk began to say their names. With each name said a

Innocence and Fatigues

face appeared in Bob's mind. Unfortunately he knew seven out of the ten.

"Thomas Johnson was the first one killed; he had taken over your squad after you had left."

"Lucky for you that you weren't there."

"The company ran into a regiment of N.V.A. they were pinned down most of the day and into the night.'

"We were unable to get a chopper in to get the dead and wounded out until the next day."

As Bob listened, he was thinking that he was with Setsuko, at the Museum and out for dinner that evening. The same time that Johnson was being raked across the chest by machine gun fire. And Zachary, who was wounded in the shoulder, played dead in the rice paddy for hours, as he lay right next to Johnson.

The more Bob thought about this 'god of war' the madder he became. He was festering a new mission for when he rejoin the company. He was no longer concerned with staying alive. His own life no longer held any value. He was going to face this 'god of war' with his own vengeance. Now Bob had to pack up all the good, which Setsuko had awakened in him, and placed them into his moldy duffel bag. Hoping that if he got the bag back home, someone else would have to try to awaken them.

Bob asked the clerk, "if there were any choppers going out to the company today?"

"Hang on there John Wayne," snapped the clerk.

"I don't even have you listed in the company yet."

"Tomorrow will be soon enough."

"You're sure in a hurry to put yourself back in harms way."

To change the subject Bob asked "where the battalion mess hall was", he was hungry.

The clerk gave him directions and told him there was a movie being played tonight in the main battalion area.

Later on that evening, Bob thought he would take in the movie with hopes of getting his mind off of the guys who had died, Setsuko and Su Lee. And who were the guys who were wounded? He was hoping that none of them sacrificed any body parts to this 'god of war'.

The theater was outdoors with wooden bleachers to sit on. There were about 80-100 guys in attendance waiting for the film to start. After twenty minutes into the film Bob had to leave, what if we got mortar, or came under a rocket attack. They would all be sitting ducks raced through his mind. He didn't sleep well that night. His mind kept jumping from one thought to the next. Hoping that he would be able to rest his mind on one good thought.

Bob was on the first chopper out the next morning. The company was getting a hot breakfast in the field along with the resupply. He was now looking forward to face this 'god of war'. There would be no surprises; he knew full well what he would be facing.

As the bird landed in the center of the company perimeter the guys hurried to unload the bird. He didn't recognize anyone unloading. He thought that he might have got on the wrong bird, until he saw Company B marks on the food containers. Then he recognized Lt. Campise showing the guys where to put the resupplies. Had they decided to combine A and B Company, was going through Bob's mind.

Later on as he was talking to Lt. Campise, he found out that things were not the same as when he left. Most of the officers were new, and the new company commander was fresh out of OCS. He has only been in country for two weeks. Also the guys who were wounded on the 21st found a way not to come back to the company. Bob tried to find out more about exactly what happened on the 21st, but those who were there didn't want to talk about it. This added to Bob's long list of unanswered questions.

As Bob looked into the faces of the new guys he wondered if he looked as scared and frightened when he first arrived in country. Now that he had surrendered his life to this 'god of war'. There was no more fear in him.

Once again, Bob had become accustomed to sleeping on the ground and being up half the night, waiting for this 'god of war' to show his head. Never knowing when the next hot meal would be coming. He just didn't care anymore. This young man again surrendered all normal human feelings, to allow himself, to become the most feared and deadly animal in the jungle. Trying to defeat this unseen 'god of war', but only to hear his laughter. Bob felt himself being pulled deeper and deeper into the madness of this war.

To this day, Bob still wonders if there was more to the war than a handful of cooked rice on a green palm leaf, and if Setsuko kept his necklace?

The flagpole

Why I stand when I see the American flag pass by.

What do you see when you look at Old Glory? There is no right or wrong answer. Everyone has to look at the American flag through their own eyes and their own experiences. You may be very patriotic and proud to be American. You might see the beauty of the flags Stars & Stripes, or you may have never been challenged to look at the flag, any deeper then it is our countries symbol.

Now when I see the flag pass by, it may be at a Fourth of July parade. Or some sporting event. This is what I see, because these eyes have seen war.

I see the American soldier. He has come from every state in the union, he may not have a star on some concrete sidewalk in Hollywood. But there is one for him on Old Glory. That star represents the state in which he lives.

His star is placed upon a blanket of blue, inducting him into the family of royalty, which dates back to 1776. Back then the men who fought, were not any different than they are today. They came from all walks of life, rich or poor, college graduate or not. This family of royalty will defend our freedoms, that we so freely enjoy today. They will stand guard seven days a week and twentyfour hours a day. So we may enjoy living in a free nation.

When I see those white stripes, I can't help but think of all those pure and innocent young man. Who witnessed the depravity of man unfold before their eyes. Leaving their innocents on the battlefield, which they will never be able to go back to again. Coming home feeling much older than the society around them. The kid who went to war, is now a man.

Those red stripes are the blood soaked bandages of the wounded and those who have paid the ultimate sacrifice for our freedom. Freedoms that they themselves will no longer have the opportunity to enjoy. They weren't just soldiers, they were fathers, mothers, sisters and brothers. They may be gone, but in this soldier's eyes, they will never be forgotten.

I will hold our flag up high. I may be too old, to be part of the royal family any more, but I am not to old to become a flagpole. One of our most important jobs we can do, is to support our troops, and the flag. My hope for you is that, you will never have to be called on to defend this great nation, but to just support the men and women watching over the homeland today. I hope you will show your support with me, and be that flagpole. Holding our flag up high, and being respectful towards our troops and our flag.

Innocence and Fatigues

Made in the USA
Middletown, DE
18 September 2016